Copyright

Be sure to check out Mike Riley's other books:

Hollywood Murders and Scandals: Tinsel Town After Dark
"In the late afternoon, her friends recalled, Monroe began to act strangely seeming to be heavily under the influence. She made statements to friend Peter Lawford that he should tell the President goodbye and tell himself goodbye."

More Hollywood Murders and Scandals: Tinsel Town After Dark
"At some point in the night Reeves and Lemmon began to argue. As Reeves headed upstairs to his bedroom, Lemmon would later tell officers that she shouted out that he would probably shoot himself."

Murders Unsolved: Cases That Have Baffled The Authorities For Years
"The body was wrapped in a plaid blanket, and placed inside a box that had once held a baby's bassinet purchased from J.C. Penney's. The boy was clean and dry, and recently groomed. However, he looked to be undernourished. Clumps of hair found on the body suggested he had been groomed after death."

Murders Unsolved Vol. 2: More Cases That Have Baffled the Authorities for Years
"McLeod first stopped at a payphone, but he didn't have any money, and so he drove to a nearby restaurant that was just opening. They didn't have a phone, but the owner gave him money to go back and use the payphone. He drove back and called the Sarasota police. Initially he was told he had to call the county Sheriff, but he responded that he didn't have any more money for more calls and then said, "They're all dead."

America's Early Serial Killers: Five Cases of Frontier Madness

"We tend to think of those early settlers as hard working, decent people only looking for religious freedom and better opportunities for their families. However, even during those times, people existed who were depraved, evil and mentally ill. These are some of their stories."

Lost and Missing: True Stories of People Gone Missing and Never Found

"Police launched a massive search, reaching miles away from where the children were last seen in all directions. However, no evidence or any of their belongings were ever found. Even if three children could have been swept out to sea unnoticed on a crowded beach, what happened to their towels, clothes, and other items?"

Lost and Missing Vol. 2: More True Stories of People Gone Missing and Never Found

"Interestingly, it was discovered that the same day of the three women's disappearance, a concrete foundation was being poured at a hospital nearby. It would have perhaps been an ideal place to dispose of three bodies, but there is no evidence to support any such claim. It's rumoured that ground-penetrating radar discovered three anomalies in the set concrete, but it has never been dug up."

Cold Cases Solved: True Stories of Murders That Took Years or Decades to Solve

"When she had been missing for three weeks, Ridulph's tearful parents appeared on TV, pleading for their daughter's release and for her to return home unharmed. However, there would be little further development in the case for four months, until the fateful day of April 26, 1958."

Table of Contents

Introduction

We like to think that our country was founded and operates on the premise of “liberty and justice for all”. Unfortunately, that is not always the case. After more than two centuries, the ideals of our founding fathers have become a bit muddied by self-interest and social and racial inequality.

Here are several real life cases where a person was charged with a crime, tried, convicted and eventually executed! Only later after their death are they either totally exonerated or widely believed to have been completely innocent! A greater miscarriage of justice cannot be imagined!

The poor souls of these people and their loved ones must be crying out because of the injustice done to them. By describing, explaining and uncovering the facts of these cases, it is hoped that more people will become aware of these horrible mistakes, and sometimes they were downright crimes.

Ultimately it is up to you to decide the true innocence or guilt of the people in the following stories.

Josefa Rodriguez: The Only Woman Legally Hanged in Texas

Accused Name: Josefa 'Chipita' Rodriguez
Crime: Robbery and murder in the first degree
Conviction Date: August 1863
Execution Date: November 13th, 1863
Date Found Innocent: June 13th, 1985

Backstory of the Accused:
Perhaps in part due to the age of the case, most of what is known about the case of Josefa (nicknamed Chipita) Rodriguez cannot be verified. Much of her story is now lost in time and has become legend. Even her first name is not conclusively known.

More is known about where she grew up, and the political climate of the time. The town of San Patricio, Texas was first created in 1829, when the Mexican government gave permission for a settlement in the area. It was their hope that almost two hundred Irish Catholic families in the area would settle there.

Some say the settlement was doomed from the beginning. The town was involved in the conflict between Mexico and Texas, and in 1836 most of the residents fled during the Battle of San Patricio. It was not until 1845 that people started to live in the town again, with the arrival of General Zachary Taylor.

San Patricio began to develop into somewhat of a rest stop for travelers. Along with the prosperity from those passing through came outlaws, traders and saloons.

Rodriguez was most likely born on December 30th, 1799. She is believed to be the child of Pedro Rodriguez, who fled from Antonio Lopez de Santa Anna, moving with Rodriguez to Texas when she was still very young. There are some reports that his wife died as they were leaving, and he and his daughter had to leave her body behind.

There are also reports that he then died fighting in the Texas Revolution, leaving Rodriguez alone in the world. It is not known exactly how old Rodriguez was when this occurred, but it's likely that for some of her life at least relative strangers raised her.

In her shack along the Aransas River, Rodriguez was known in the area for providing meals and a place to sleep to travelers of the Cotton Road. Both traveling cowboys and those from perhaps the darker side of life enjoyed her hospitality. Rodriguez reportedly knew how to handle herself, and made a good living from her venture.

There were rumors in the town that a man employed as Rodriguez's hired help, Juan Silvera, was in fact her illegitimate son. Perhaps her own childhood led her to become an unwed mother in the 1800's. He was reportedly the son of a drifter or trader in the town that Rodriguez took up with, only to be abandoned again when he moved on without them. Silvera's mental faculties have also been called into question, with some reporting him as a 'half wit'.

Rodriguez continued to operate her makeshift inn well into her sixties, which is where the story of her alleged crime begins.

Description of the Crime:
In 1863, Rodriguez took in a man named John Savage. Savage was a traveling horse trader, and arrived at Rodriguez's place looking for a meal and board for the night. His saddlebags were noticeably full. What a casual observer did not know is that they were filled with hundreds of pieces of gold. The gold's worth was estimated at $600, which would be worth over $17,000 today, certainly enough to provide a motive for a single woman living in poverty to commit murder.

Two servants from a nearby ranch first found Savage's body. The women were washing clothing in the river when they found a burlap bag floating down the stream. They managed to drag the bag ashore, and when they opened it, they must have gotten the shock of their lives, for in the bag they found the hacked remains of Savage.

His head had been split open by an axe. Then his body was placed in the burlap bag and sent down the river. Curiously, all of his gold was also found lying downriver. When investigators searched Rodriguez's house, she did not have any of the gold in her possession, nor any other of Savage's personal items.

Evidence Used to Convict:
Rodriguez had noticed that Savage was gone when she arose in the morning, but reportedly had simply assumed he had left before the sun rose.

When the Sheriff visited Rodriguez's property, he found blood on the porch, which Rodriguez told him was chicken blood. Of course, in 1863, they could not even dream of the scientific technology we have available today to be able to test that claim.

Searching her home, investigators discovered the alleged murder weapon. They determined that the axe used to hack Savage to death was in fact the same one that Rodriguez used to split kindling. There was little other evidence found, but law enforcement officers arrested both Rodriguez and Silvera for the murder of Savage.

Rodriguez would say nothing to the Sheriff at all regarding the murder or the discovery of Savage's body. Silvera reportedly told him that he had helped Rodriguez dump the body in the river. However, this was only after significant prodding by the Sheriff. If Silvera was indeed mentally disabled, can his testimony even be believed?

Most of the evidence presented at Rodriguez's trial was circumstantial. It is not known if Rodriguez was even aware of what Savage carried in his saddlebags, but the prosecutors told the jury that she had fixed her eyes upon obtaining his riches from the moment he arrived at her makeshift inn. It was the prosecution's contention that Rodriguez, along with Silvera, had murdered Savage, with robbery on their minds. Despite this, law enforcement recovered the entire amount of gold just downstream from the body, completely untouched.

Rodriguez did not say a word the entire trial, even refusing to testify in her own defense. Because of this, many in the community felt that while she was innocent herself, she knew who the guilty party was. There were whispers that in fact, Silvera was the only one who used the axe around the property, and he committed the murder alone. If he were, indeed, Rodriguez's son, this would give her an obvious reason to protect him.

The trial lasted not even a single day. It began in the morning and by lunch the jury returned a guilty verdict. Despite their verdict, perhaps the jury also was not 100% convinced, as they recommended leniency for Rodriguez alone, excluding Silvera from their recommendation.

The judge presiding over the case, Benjamin F. Neal, ignored the request and sentenced Rodriguez to death by hanging.

The jury found Silvera guilty of second-degree murder, and the judge sentenced him to just five years in jail.

From the day her sentence was handed down to the day it was carried out, Rodriguez was held at the home of the local Sheriff, William Means. During this time, there were two lynch mob attempts on her life, but both were thwarted. Another record tells that Rodriguez was kept in leg irons and shackled to a wall in the courthouse.

Stories indicate that the locals felt sorry for her. Local children would bring her candy and supplies to make cigarettes. Transcripts report that a local woman refused the use of her wagon to transport Rodriguez to the scene of her execution.

Just before her execution, the women of the town washed Rodriguez, braided her hair and gave her a dress to wear, which was reportedly quite beautiful and not at all a simple gown. It is also known that prominent citizens in the town urged the Sheriff to not carry out the execution. Perhaps feeling the pressure, the day before the execution, the Sheriff left the town, leaving the hangman to carry out the sentence alone.

Ironically, Rodriguez was executed on the banks of the same river in which Savage's body was found. It was the only place that had a tree high enough to carry out the sentence. Just before her she died, Rodriguez finally spoke, saying only one thing; "No soy culpable", I am not guilty.

It's reported that the oxen moving the wagon underneath her moved so slowly that Rodriguez's neck did not snap, and instead she slowly strangled to death. Many at the scene were strongly affected, with women fainting and children running away crying. Even one man turned away, saying he could not handle seeing any more.

At least one witness to her death reported hearing a moan come from her coffin, well after Rodriguez was pronounced dead. She was buried along the banks of the same river in an unmarked grave.

How Innocence Was Confirmed:

Except for a single week of transcripts, nearly the entire record of Rodriguez's case was lost in either a fire or flood at some unknown point in history. What can still be determined from the remaining records is that no official jury was ever empanelled. Instead, the Sheriff instructed the jury foreman to find at least twenty other qualified men, women not being allowed to serve on a jury at that point in history.

It's reported that he returned with closer to thirty men, some with serious conflicts of interest. At least three members of the 'jury' had also been on the grand jury that had initially indicted her on the same charges. Perhaps amazingly, the foreman of that grand jury had been the Sheriff himself! It's likely that the Sheriff's instructions to the new foreman to find others to serve on the trial greatly biased the jury against Rodriguez. As well as the unorthodox way the jury was selected, other members of both juries had also been indicted with felonies themselves, including one for murder.

There is also evidence that Rodriguez's ethnic background influenced how swiftly she was arrested and convicted. Some believe that had she not been 'Mexican' (as she was referred to in reports of the day) she would never have even been indicted, much less found guilty. Newspapers of the time even complimented the jury for finding Rodriguez guilty, saying that 'Mexicans should not have the same rights in this state as Americans'.

Rodriguez defense was also very weak. She had little in the way of counsel herself, and her sole statement at trial was her plea of not guilty. There was not a single appeal or motion made on her behalf during the trial, and talk of a retrial after she was found guilty never turned into anything more than gossip.

As well as rumors regarding the protection of her son, other sources also report that she was in fact involved in gathering information for the state regarding the Civil War, and that she was framed as a political act.

In 1985, more than one hundred years after her conviction and death, Texan state senator Carlos Truan asked the state legislature to absolve Rodriguez of murder. On June 13, 1985, Governor Mark White signed the resolution.

Current Status:
For many years, Rodriguez was considered to be the only woman to be legally hanged by the state of Texas. Rodriguez's case has been the subject of multiple works of fiction and non-fiction, including operas, books, magazines and newspaper stories.

Unsurprisingly, her tale has also developed into a ghost story. Many believe her spirit walks along the banks of the river to this day, her mournful cries carried on the wind. Her burial place is said by some to have caused her ghost to wander, having not been buried in a cemetery in sacred ground. It is said that the cry pierces the night air, and freezes the blood of any who hear it. The story tells that her ghost is particularly active when another woman is to be executed, her ghost appearing as a specter with the noose still around her neck.

Perhaps fittingly, the date of Rodriguez's hanging was Friday November 13th, 1863.

Joe Hill: A Labor Organizer Martyred

Accused Name: Joe Hill
Crime: Murder
Conviction Date: July 18th, 1914
Execution Date: November 19th, 1915
Date Found Innocent: Never officially exonerated but widely considered innocent

Backstory of the Accused:
Joe Hill was born Joel Emmanuel Haaglund, in Sweden in 1879. Born to parents Olaf and Margareta, he was the third child in a family of nine siblings. Three of his siblings died when they were young, a sad but common occurrence in those times.

His father a conductor on the railway line died at forty-one years of age in 1887. His death was a huge blow financially to his family, but his mother still managed to keep the family together until her own death in 1902, when Hill was in his early twenties.

Around the same time, Hill became very ill himself with tuberculosis. He underwent extensive treatment in Stockholm, Sweden's capital city. Then, in 1902 he immigrated to the USA with his brother Paul. It was here that he changed his name to Joseph Hillstrom, or Joe Hill.

Hill first settled in New York, on the lower East Bowery. At first he was excited about the promise of the fairytale American Dream, but soon discovered the harsh and often exploitative conditions that migrant workers frequently experienced. Those experiences would lead him down a path that likely led ultimately to his death.

After living for a time in New York, Hill then traveled to Cleveland, Ohio and then onto the west coast. He was in San Francisco in 1906 and experienced the devastating earthquake that killed over 3,000 people.

Hill worked as a miner, in the lumber industry, and as a longshoreman. By 1910, he was working in California on the docks. He joined the Industrial Workers of the World (IWW), an international radical labor union. The group has ties to both socialist and anarchist labor movements, and still exists today. Hill rose through the organization, and traveled widely under their banner.

Back then, there was certainly no love lost between the union and people who supported a strictly capitalist society. Hill was very active in the union, writing both political songs and poetry, and also made speeches. It was here that he primarily started using the shortened version of his name, Joe Hill, as a pen name. A practice of anti-union blacklisting existed, and it is likely Hill shortened his name so as to be able to continue to find work as Joseph Hillstrom.

Hill often used popular melodies from the time as a basis for his songs, and even coined the now well-known phrase 'pie in the sky'. His work became famous worldwide, and was used at drives and rallies supporting strikes. Hill himself was also often involved in organized meetings and protests of the group.

Hill was an itinerant worker, and traveled to find work often also. He would often hop freight trains to travel from job to job. His travels and activities were not always smooth sailing. In 1912 he was assaulted at a free speech campaign in San Diego, leaving him permanently scarred. Eventually his involvement with the union made finding work in California extremely difficult, and so he moved on. In 1913, he was working in Park City, Utah, as a laborer in the Silver King Mine.

Description of the Crime:
In 1913 Hill was attending a successful strike at the United Construction Company, one that he was likely also involved in organizing in the first place. During the strike

Hill lived with some friends from Salt Lake City, in nearby Park City.

While he was there, on January 10th, 1914, a former policeman named J.B. Morrison was shot and killed in a grocery store by two masked gunmen. The two men were described as being armed, with faces covered by red bandanas.

Just a few weeks prior, Morrison had told a journalist that he had been threatened with a revenge attack from an incident that occurred when he was in the police force. Acting on the theory of a revenge attack the police originally identified several men as suspects. Perhaps incredibly, a full twelve other people were arrested in the case before Hill was even approached.

The same night as the murder of Morrison, Hill had visited a doctor with a bullet wound of his own. He had been shot and left with a wound in his left lung, from an argument over a woman, the doctor was told. Despite that, given that the bullet had passed cleanly through Hill, the doctor informed the police of the wound, also telling police that Hill had been armed with a pistol of his own when he saw him.

Evidence Used to Convict:
When the police were informed of Hill's injury, it quickly brought suspicion on Hill for Morrison's murder. The police were already aware of Hill's union actions and affiliations. Adding to this a witness told police he heard one of Morrison's attackers proclaim, "Oh God, I'm shot." Based on this circumstantial evidence, Hill was arrested and charged with murder.

Police claim to have found a red bandana in Hill's room, and the pistol reported by the doctor missing. Hill denied any involvement, claiming that his hands were over his head when he was shot. A bullet hole in his coat indicated his position and seemed to corroborate Hill's statement.

The evidence at trial seemed to be strongly on Hill's side. None of the witnesses were able to identify him conclusively as one of the attackers. No evidence of the bullet that passed through Hill was found in the store, nor was any of his blood found at the scene.

Given the preponderance of evidence seemingly on his side, Hill is believed to have thought that he should not have to testify on principle, believing he could never be convicted with such a limited amount of evidence against him.

Hill never did testify at the trial, and his lawyers told the court that there were four other people treated for gunshot wounds in Salt Lake City that night alone. Prior to being arrested for his murder, Hill had no prior links or connections to Morrison. The defense's position was the lack of a robbery at the store and Hill's otherwise unfamiliarity with Morrison left the prosecution with no motive to support the charge.

No money had been taken from the store and another witness heard one of the attackers say to Morrison "We've got you now". This supported Morrison's own statement that someone was after him for revenge.

The prosecution did produce twelve witnesses, all who testified that the killer resembled Hill. Morrison's brother at first proclaimed, "That's not him at all" when first laying eyes on Hill. The same man would later identify Hill positively as the murderer.

After only a couple hours' deliberation by the jury and despite the lack of any conclusive evidence Hill was found guilty of murder. He was then sentenced to death. His lawyers attempted to appeal to the Utah Supreme Court, but they were unsuccessful.

Orrin N. Hilton, the lawyer representing Hill for the appeal, claimed that all it took was the court knowing of Hill's involvement in the IWW for them to assume guilt. He blamed the press for forcing Hill's associations into the trial.

Hill refused to explain the origins of his own wound further at trial or appeal, which did not help his cause. A Chief Justice wrote that the wound was a distinguishing mark and by remaining silent the defendant could not avoid the natural and reasonable inferences. A socialist newspaper proclaimed that the murder of Morrison demanded a scapegoat, and as a member of the IWW who was not born in America, Hill was the perfect foil.

His case created a worldwide protest, as unionists and others learned of the trial and verdict. A petition with more than 30,000 member signatures was sent to then Governor, William Spry, calling on him to free Hill.

Famous people, including Helen Keller, the Swedish Ambassador, and the public from countries worldwide called for clemency. Even President Woodrow Wilson called for Hill to be granted a retrial.

Many believed that the case was used as an excuse to get rid of Hill by the mine owners and other wealthy citizens of the city. While there is no direct evidence to prove this theory, there is no doubt that the opinion in Utah, and over the West, was extremely hostile towards the IWW union and Hill.

Despite all these efforts, a date was set for Hill's execution. He was set to die by firing squad on November 19th, 1915. When the news of his impending execution reached Hill, he sent a message to the union leader, Bill Haywood, telling him that he would die like a true rebel. He told them not to waste any time in mourning, but to continue to 'organize' (continue the union's work and protests). He did not want to be buried in Utah, and asked Haywood to arrange for him to be buried over state lines. Before he died, he wrote his last work, a poem called My Last Will.

On the day of the execution, Hill himself called out to the squad to go ahead and fire. That day, a bomb was found at the estate of the owner of Standard Oil Company. Police believe the IWW planted the bomb as a protest against the execution.

Over 30,000 people attended Hill's funeral. Following his wishes expressed to his friends in arms and in the poem My Last Will, his body was transported to Chicago, where it was cremated. His ashes were then distributed within six hundred envelopes and sent all around the world, to be scattered on the wind in every state in the union, and several other countries as well.

How Innocence Was Confirmed:
Today, it is obvious that under current laws, Hill would have never been convicted, let alone executed. The evidence was overwhelmingly circumstantial, and Hill had more than enough evidence on his side to create reasonable doubt in a modern court of law. However, Hill has never been officially cleared of his conviction.

Current Status:
Since his execution, Hill has become both a martyr and hero for the labor movement, and a symbol of the fight for justice for the disadvantaged. Many of his songs and poetry works are still in use today.

The house where Hill grew up still stands today in Gavle a province of Gastrikland in Sweden. In 2011 it became a museum and garden, and hosts cultural events.

A modern day biographer for Hill, William M. Adler, believes that although he was most likely innocent of murder, he came to see himself as worth more to the labor movement as a martyr than when he was alive. He believes this influenced Hill's decision not to testify at his own trial.

After his death, a letter written by Hill's sweetheart, Hilda Erikson, surfaced potentially explaining what truly did happen to Hill on the night he was shot. In 1949, Erikson wrote to a professor named Aubrey Haan, who was researching a book about Hill's life. Haan did not end up publishing the book, but another biographer, William Adler then found the letter in Haan's research.

It seems that Hill had been a victim of love, shot by Erikson's ex fiancé, who was competing with Hill for Erikson's affections. At the time Erikson, who was in her early twenties, was much younger than the thirty-six year old Hill and was the niece of two Swedish brothers Hill was boarding with. He refused to admit the cause of his bullet wound so as to protect her identity from the public.

A career criminal named Frank Z. Wilson is today recognized as the most likely suspect for the murder. He was seen walking without an overcoat near the grocery store on the night of Morrison's murder, and was also in possession of a bloody handkerchief.

Wilson is on record as having repeatedly lied to police over various investigations, and has been known to use more than sixteen aliases over multiple arrests and convictions in his lifetime, including involvement in the St. Valentine's Day Massacre.
A small amount of Hill's ashes remain, and have been interred in Sweden, as well as being used in other ceremonies surrounding IWW members, as late as 1989.

Over the years there have been many different pieces of work created around Hill's life, including plays, biographies, songs, books, and movies. A popular American folk song "I Dreamed I Saw Joe Hill Last Night" was written in 1936, at

Camp Unity, a celebration of his life and his works. Most famously, Joan Baez sang the song at Woodstock, and brought it and Hill's cause to the attention of the world.

With the evidence only being circumstantial and the multitudes who believed in his innocence, who's to say if justice was done.

Joe Arridy: Died Without Understanding Why

Accused Name: Joe Arridy
Crime: Assault, Rape, and Murder
Conviction Date: April 17th, 1937
Execution Date: January 6th, 1939
Date Found Innocent: January 7th, 2011

Backstory of the Accused:
Joe Arridy was born on April 29th, 1915 in Pueblo, Colorado. His parents were Syrian immigrants, and did not speak English themselves. Arridy started attending public school at Bessemer Elementary, but by the time Arridy entered the second grade, the principal called his parents to the school and told them Arridy could not continue, as he 'could not learn'.

For the next three years, Arridy's parents kept him at home. It's reported that he was a passive but happy child, enjoying playing by himself the most. His favorite activity was making mud pies.

By age ten, Arridy was living a state home for the mentally disabled, in Grand Junction, Colorado. Tests showed that he was unable to recall and repeat four numbers, identify colors, and spoke only in incomplete, short sentences. His IQ was said to be just 46. As at home, his institution reports list no incidents. For the most part, Arridy was a quiet loner.

Arridy continued to live at the institution for another nine months, at which time his father requested that Arridy be returned to live with them. The request was granted and he would live at home for the next three years. Arridy continued to enjoy his own company more than that of others, and would often take long walks alone around town.

When he was fourteen years old, a probation officer found

a gang of other boys performing sexual acts on Arridy. The officer reported the incident to the court, labeling Arridy as 'one of the worst mental defective cases I have ever seen'. The court responded by ordering Arridy immediately return to live at the institution. He continued to live there for the next seven years.

Records report that he was unable to work on the institution's farm, nor attend school. He was given the 'job' of working with the kindergarten teacher. She reported that Arridy was only capable of performing simple, short tasks, such as washing the dishes or running small errands. In her opinion, he was totally dependent on others for any leadership or suggestions.

By the time Arridy was twenty-two years of age, he would go with other institution inmates to watch men riding on the top of railroad boxcars on trains that passed by the institution. One day, they left the grounds together, jumped on the boxcars themselves, and took a full day's ride throughout the mountains, eventually arriving in Pueblo, Arridy's hometown. They then immediately started the same journey back again.

Arridy was seen in Grand Junction on August 13th, 1936. It's believed that he then jumped a boxcar either that night or early the next morning. He wasn't seen again until he walked up to the kitchen car of a railway workers gang in Cheyenne, Wyoming. It was August 20th, and Arridy was both dirty and hungry.

Description of the Crime:

On Saturday August 15th, 1936, or possibly just after midnight the next day, two sisters Dorothy (15) and Barbara (12) Drain were both beaten severely while sleeping in the same bed at their home in Pueblo. Dorothy was also raped and died from her injuries. Barbara, while grievously injured, survived.

On August 26th, Arridy was arrested by two railroad detectives, and turned over to Sheriff George Carroll. Along with other law enforcement officers in towns all around the area, Carroll was actively picking up multiple suspects and then interrogating them in relation to the attack and murder of the Drain girls.

Carroll questioned Arridy for an hour and a half, at which time he called a reporter and told him that he had been given a full confession for the crimes. At least one reporter has since said that Carroll then recited a series of long, complex statements that were allegedly direct quotes from Arridy, a man who according to his mental institution records, could barely speak in a complete sentence. Carroll claimed Arridy was the sole perpetrator, and had bludgeoned the girls with a club.

Receipt of the confession came as a shock to the police back in Pueblo, as they already had their own suspect in custody. They had also recovered the actual murder weapon, the head of an axe that matched the wound patterns from the girls. The suspect was Frank Aguilar, and as he was professing his innocence, all evidence was carefully catalogued and kept. Unlike Arridy, Aguilar had a connection to the victims. He was a former WPA worker, and his boss was the Drain sister's father.

When Sheriff Carroll found out about Aguilar, he changed his story. He interrogated Arridy again, and this time told reporters that an axe had been used by Arridy to commit the attack. He also now reported that Arridy had committed the crime in corroboration with Aguilar.

Evidence Used to Convict:

Carroll maintained full control over Arridy's arrest and investigation into his guilt. When two detectives from Pueblo arrived in Cheyenne, they were added to Carroll's investigative team, with him continuing to lead it. When Arridy was taken to Pueblo, Carroll was the one to transport him. He was also present at the Pueblo Police Station, where Arridy and Aguilar allegedly met each other.

He continued to maintain his hold over the investigation when Arridy was taken to the Drain home, and at the prison where Aguilar signed a confession that included Arridy's initials in a lower left column, almost as a side note. The confession was published in the newspaper, but was later withdrawn and never presented in court.

Arridy's trial began on December 15th, four months to the day since the crime occurred. It lasted just seven days.

It seems almost incredible today, but no recordings or paper records existed of Carroll's interrogations of Arridy, nor did Arridy ever sign a confession or other document, other than his alleged initialing of Aguilar's non-presented confession. Carroll dictated Arridy's alleged confession and interrogation statements daily to the media. During Arridy's trial, Carroll became the prosecution's star witness. According to reports of the day, Carroll testified entirely from memory, not referring to a single note during his long statements to the court.

Carroll ended up taking the stand five different times for the prosecution. Court transcripts show that Carroll testified at length without interruption or question, almost as if he was telling a riveting story. He testified that Arridy was in complete control of his own mental faculties, and spoke to him in clear sentences regarding intimate details surrounding the case, such as the color of the girl's nightgowns.

Arridy's defense argued pre-trial that he should be found not guilty for reasons of insanity. In other interviews not conducted by Carroll, Arridy did not know who Roosevelt was (the President at the time), nor did he seem to know what the alleged murder weapon, a hatchet, even was. He also seemed to not recognize that his own father was present in the courtroom.

The defense argued that Arridy had no capacity to discern right from wrong. While three separate psychologists testified that Arridy did not have this ability, they also said that Arridy was also not insane. They claimed that for one to become insane, they must have at one time been normal, and that Arridy had never been normal.

In modern times, this seems like a strange distinction, but protection for the mentally disabled was far less than today. In fact, it was only nine years earlier than a ruling had been issued allowing the forced sterilization of mentally disabled people.

During the pre-trial hearing, the jury at first deadlocked, but then just one hour later voted that Arridy should stand trial for murder.

Another occurrence that seems extremely strange to us today was that Arridy's defense conducted absolutely no independent investigation into the crime. He announced at the start of the trial that he would only be cross-examining prosecution witnesses, and would not present his own evidentiary defense.

The defense also requested that the earlier sanity verdict be set aside, and that the court allow him to argue the case again at this trial. He requested that the judge allow him to make his opening statement only after the prosecution had presented their entire evidentiary case. Perhaps he believed that Arridy's best case at acquittal was to prove that he did not have the mental capacity to commit the crime.

The judge granted all the defense motions, and this time four psychologists, the same three and one more, testified on Arridy's behalf. However, they gave the same testimony as the pre-trial hearing.

When Carroll testified, the defense allowed him to continue unchallenged. When he was cross-examined, Carroll boasted of his thirty years experience, claiming that he spent seven hours with Arridy in interrogation. The defense then asked him if he believed Arridy could distinguish right from wrong. Carroll responded that he had no doubt whatsoever that he could.

Along with Carroll's testimony, a single hair was 'matched' to Arridy's. However, the chain of custody was not preserved properly on the hair. Matching a hair to an individual without DNA is a questionable technique even today, let alone in the 1930's.

On April 17th, 1937, Arridy was found guilty and sentenced to death. And yet, the astonishing details of this case were not over. On August 13th, before the court handed down Arridy's sentence, Aguilar, who had also been found guilty of the same murder, was executed for the crime. That same day, Carroll, along with two railroad detectives, received a $1000 reward for Arridy's arrest.

Many believed it to be a miscarriage of justice that Arridy was ever convicted. Lawyer Gail Ireland fought on Arridy's behalf for over a year and a half, and over that time managed to win at least six stays of execution. However it could not be stopped indefinitely. On January 6th, 1939, the Colorado Supreme Court voted to deny the petition, and the Governor told the prison to carry out Arridy's execution. The judges' vote was extremely close, the petition was denied by just a single vote.

That night, the chaplain administered the last rights for a child. On the way to his execution, Arridy gave away to another prisoner his toy train. It had been given to him by the warden, and was his most prized possession. During the long days on death row, Arridy would wind the train up, and then send it chugging down the corridor. Other inmates would stretch out their hands, causing both wrecks and then rescues that made Arridy laugh aloud. They would then wind up the train themselves and send it back to its carefree owner for another trip.

According to the media reports, after giving away his train, Arridy then 'walked to his death with the faith of a child'.

How Innocence Was Confirmed:
In 1995, interest in Arridy's case was reignited when Denver native and advocate for the mentally disabled, Robert Perske, published a book that included Arridy's case. Perske states that he has worked on many cases, and the trial and execution of Arridy was the worst miscarriage of justice he has ever seen.

Then, Denver attorney David Martinez started to gather research to formally request a pardon for Arridy from the Governor. A support organization that works with the mentally disabled were also working to clear Arridy's name.

Only a handful of pardons have ever been given in death penalty cases across the entire USA. On January 7th, 2011, Colorado Governor Bill Ritter officially pardoned Arridy. A bit too little, too late?

Current Status:
At Frank Aguilar's trial, Barbara Drain identified him as her and her sister's attacker. She did not even attend Arridy's trial, let alone identify him.

Sheriff Carroll was involved in the group that brought down the notorious Barker gang, a gang active during the Depression and recognized as one of the most ruthless. He was famous for being particularly loquacious and liked to brag about his involvement in bringing down the gang.

After Arridy's death sentence had already been handed

down, Mrs. R. O. McMurtree identified Aguilar as the sole attacker in another crime that happened just two weeks prior and three blocks away from the attack on the Drain sisters. McMurtee, 58, was sleeping in the same bed as her 72-year-old aunt when Aguilar attacked them both, beating them just as the Drain girls were. McMurtee's aunt also died from her injuries.

Today the death penalty is banned in many states for those with serious mental limitations.

Gail Ireland, who fought tirelessly for Arridy's life, became the Colorado Attorney General. In a letter to a friend, Ireland wrote that the state of Colorado would be committing murder itself if it were to execute Arridy.

In the cemetery where Arridy is buried, many graves of prisoners are not even marked with names, and many are overgrown with weeds. However Arridy's grave is nearly pristine, and marked by a two-foot tall headstone. The headstone is carved with his name, date of death, and includes a picture of Arridy with his beloved toy train. Laid only in 2007, it's proof that nearly eighty years after his death, Joe Arridy still has friends keeping him in their thoughts.

A little known poem by Margeurite Young describes a warden weeping as he watches a condemned man put to death. The poem is what first drew Perske to look into Arridy's case, haunting him with its somber words. A verse reads:

"The man you kill tonight is six years old,
He has no idea why he dies,
Yet he must die in the room the state has walled
Transparent to its glassy eyes."

Margeurite Young

George Stinney: Too Young, Too Fast

Accused Name: George Stinney
Crime: Murder
Conviction Date: April 24th, 1944
Execution Date: June 16th, 1944
Date Found Innocent: December 17th, 2014

Backstory of the Accused:
George Stinney, Jr. was born on October 21st, 1929. He was African-American and lived with his family in South Carolina, in the small segregated town of Alcolu. Stinney's father worked in the local mill. At the time of the crime and his arrest, Stinney was just fourteen years old, 90 pounds, and barely five feet tall. He was reportedly illiterate.

At the time, the population of the town was approximately 1,700 people. In recent history, Alcolu has produced five governors of South Carolina.

Originally a company town, the vast majority of Alcolu's citizens worked at one of the companies owned by D.W. Alderman & Sons. The businesses included a sawmill, planing mill, hosiery mill, and flooring mill, plus farming and cattle ranching. The company also owned a cotton gin, hotel, store, and several other businesses.

As the town grew, the company built schools, churches, telephone and electricity plants, and sporting grounds. It paid company employees in 'babbits', which could be used in the company stores.

Alcolu was a segregated town, with the two churches known as the 'black church' and the 'white church'.

In 1947, just a few years after Stinney's death, the Alderman family sold the lumber mill to another company. Eventually in the year 2000 it was closed. Today the population of Alcolu is just 429. The only thing that remains of the mill is an old storage shed, half swallowed by weeds.

Description of the Crime:
March 23rd, 1944 was a beautiful sunny spring day in Alcolu. The small community was a quiet and friendly one, and rarely was any violent crime committed. That afternoon, two white girls named Betty June Binnicker (11) and Mary Emma Thames (8), were beaten to death, their bodies left lying in a ditch.

Binnicker and Thames had gone for a walk to pick flowers, taking Binnicker's bicycle with them, which they rode along the railway tracks. The girls often walked through this area of town. As they walked along the path, they came across a young black man, Stinney, who was at the time fourteen. The girls both knew Stinney, it was almost impossible not to know everyone else in the small town.

Within a few hours of the girls leaving to go walking, their families were already frantic when they did not return. It was very unusual for them not to return home at the appointed time, and their knowledge of the local area made it unlikely that they were simply lost.

The local lumber mill organized a search party. Although they searched through the night no trace of the girls was found. It would not be until the next day that a searcher would find small footprints. Following the prints, they soon came across a pair of scissors, recognized as Binnickers, taken along to cut flowers. Within minutes of the find, the search party found the girl's bodies, lying in a muddy ditch, obscured by thick thorny bushes. The girls' bodies were found just a few minutes walk from the 'black church'. The fact that the bodies of two white girls were found on 'the black side of town' was scandalous.

Both girls had been brutally beaten. Binnicker had severe wounds on the back of her skull, while Thames had five separate skull fractures.

Evidence Used to Convict:
Once their bodies were found, it did not take long for Stinney to be arrested for their murder. He had been part of the search team, and during the search had told another member of the team that he had spoken to the girls before they disappeared.

Stinney was arrested at his family's home. He was found hiding behind the chicken coop terrified when two big black cars drove up to their house. Neither parent was home when white law enforcement officers handcuffed the fourteen year old and took him and his stepbrother, Johnny.

Johnny was later released from custody. Stinney's sister Aime, who followed him around so much that he called her his shadow, asked Stinney where he was going. Stinney told her to find his parents and tell them he had been taken away. That was the last time she would ever see her brother alive.

Once he was arrested, although he was only fourteen years old, Stinney was interrogated without his parents being present. The questioning went on for hours, and was conducted by several white police officers. Eventually, a deputy claimed that Stinney had told him that he wanted to have sex with Binnicker, and had to kill Thames to be able to do this. When Thames refused to leave them alone, he then killed both the girls for refusing his advances.

It is not known how valid this confession was, some reports state that Stinney was offered an ice cream cone in return for his confession. There is no official record of the confession ever existing.

On March 26th, just after Stinney's arrest, a mob of 1,500 white citizens gathered at the jail in an attempt to administer mob justice. Deputies then moved Stinney to a more secure location.

Stinney was also not allowed to see his parents at all after his arrest, even before he went to trial. He went to face twelve white men alone.

It was alleged that Stinney was one of the last people to see the girls alive, the prosecution stating that they had passed by his home and asked him where they could find a particular type of flower.

Stinney's trial was, at best, poorly run. No physical evidence tying him to the crime was presented, and no witnesses were called. His lawyer was a tax lawyer, and did not appeal the trial's verdict. Two conflicting confessions allegedly by Stinney were both entered into evidence.

In the first he claimed he struck the girls in self-defense, after they attacked him when he was trying to help them after they had fallen into a ditch. In the second, he allegedly followed the girls into the woods and attacked Thames first, then chased Binnicker and killed her also.

The court also allowed the admission of the 'possibility' of rape, based only on a slight swelling and bruise on the external genitalia of Binnicker. There was no other physical evidence, and both girls' hymens were intact.

His lawyer's only defense was that Stinney was too young to be considered responsible for his crimes. However in South Carolina at the time, a person was considered to be an adult when they reached the age of fourteen. Stinney was fourteen years and five months old at the time of the offence.

The courthouse was bursting at the seams, with over 1,500 people coming to witness the proceedings. The entire event lasted only two hours, and the jury then deliberated for a ridiculous ten minutes before finding Stinney guilty and sentencing him to death.

Stinney's parents were only allowed to see him once, after the trial was already over. They were convinced he was innocent, but as a poor black family living in the South, they had little recourse to challenge the verdict.

His family was also terrified of someone taking revenge against the family. While lynchings were rare in the 1940's, violence and vigilantism against blacks in the South was recent enough for it to still be a clear threat in his parent's memories.

It's reported that the National Association for the Advancement of Colored People (NAACP) tried to intervene in Stinney's case, but were not successful.

Stinney was put to death by electric chair on July 16th, 1944. He was so small that the seat had to be stacked with books to enable him to fit the equipment. Even so, during the execution the mask slipped off, allowing witnesses to see the agony on the fourteen year old's face. It took several jolts for him to eventually die.

How Innocence Was Confirmed:
Stinney's family spent years trying to get his case officially re-opened. They argued that his confession had been coerced. The family wrote to famous activists and celebrities, including Oprah Winfrey for support.

In 2004 George Frierson became interested in the case. Frierson was a local historian and member of the school district. He was also born in Alcolu, and went to elementary school there. The more Frierson investigated, the more he became convinced of Stinney's innocence.

His research caught the interest of attorneys Steve McKenzie and Matt Burgess. They took up the case on behalf of the Stinney family. The pair filed papers in October 2013, requesting that the verdict be overturned.

Along with Miller Shealy, a professor of criminal procedure, they presented evidence that included sworn statements from Stinney's siblings. A man who had been in prison with Stinney revealed that Stinney told him he had been forced to confess. Stinney's sister, Aime Ruffner, testified that Stinney had been with her at the time the girls were murdered. This was never brought up at his original trial.

Aime says that her story has not changed in seventy years, though at the hearing prosecutors accused her of not properly remembering details of a statement she had given in 2009.

She said that the memory of seeing the girls with Stinney that day was completely clear in her mind as it was so unusual to see any white people on that side of town. After asking where they could find a particular plant, they moved on, and Stinney stayed with her.

Reverend Francis Batson, who pulled the girl's bodies from the water-filled ditch, also presented an affidavit. He stated that there was hardly any blood around the bodies or in the ditch, which indicated that the girls were likely killed elsewhere, given the extent of their injuries. Their bodies would have to have been moved and left in the ditch after their deaths. Frierson questioned how Stinney, who was only 95 pounds, would have even been able to move the girls' bodies.

Despite this, there was still resistance against overturning the verdict among the white population of Alcolu. Some have claimed that Stinney was a bully, with one person telling the local paper that he had once threatened to kill her. However, most believe that in a segregated Southern town in the 1940's, it would be rare for a black boy to ever threaten a white child without strong repercussions.

Stinney's seventh grade teacher, who was also black, reported that Stinney had a temper and had gotten into a fight with a girl at school, injuring her with a knife. Stinney's family claims the report is a lie.

On Wednesday, December 17th, 2014, Judge Carmen Mullins vacated the verdict against Stinney, seventy years after he was put to death. She claimed that no one could justify a fourteen-year-old child being arrested, tried, convicted, and then executed all in just eighty days.

She also referenced the lack of performance of Stinney's defense attorney, who called no witnesses, presented no evidence, asked no questions during cross examination, and failed to submit an appeal.

Stinney's lawyer had been running for office at the time of the trial. Had he been motivated to not anger the white citizens of the town, rather than provide a proper defense for Stinney? Judge Mullins also criticized other aspects of the case, such as a witness who discovered the girl's bodies being allowed to sit in on the coroner's inquest.

Stinney's sister, Katherine Robinson, now eighty years old, said about Judge Mullin's ruling that, "It was like a cloud just moved away".

Current Status:
The day Stinney was arrested, his father was fired from his job at the mill, and the family was run out of town. Seventy years later, Stinney's sister Aime says she has never returned.

Binnicker's family remains convinced of Stinney's guilt. The family had already lost one child as an infant, and then would go on to lose a son in the Korean War, and so perhaps that influenced their thoughts on Binniker's tragic death.

They insist that there were absolutely no racial factors in Stinney's trial, and believe that the lawyers defending

Stinney's case in modern times were motivated by money, stating they claimed that they would sue the state for wrongful death if Stinney's verdict were vacated.

A cousin of the Binniker family is more sympathetic, believing that Stinney should have had a parent or lawyer with him during the investigation, and that he should never have been executed, despite the guilty verdict.

The lawyers working on Stinney's pardon claim that the money would only be used to cover legal fees, with the remaining going to a scholarship foundation, if suing for wrongful death is even possible. They believe that Stinney's confession was changed to suit the prosecution as the case went on. In 1944, it's likely that the police put many different scenarios to Stinney, who simply answered 'Yes, Sir' when told what 'happened'.

In the South Carolina State Archives there is a thick file with hundreds of letters and telegrams telling of the outrage against the execution of a minor. Some said the sentence should be commuted to life in prison, while others believed that a new investigation and trial should be held.

The Governor at the time, Olin Johnston, who was running for the US Senate, would not change his mind. Two days before the execution he wrote back to someone who had written to him asking for clemency.

He told them that Stinney had killed Thames so he could rape Binnicker, and then killed Binnicker before he raped her, returning to the body to attempt to rape her again. Johnston claimed Stinney had admitted all this, but in fact it was only rumor, and was actually contradicted by the post-mortem.

Stinney remains the youngest person to be executed in the US since the beginning of the 20th Century. In 1988, a ruling in the Supreme Court prohibited the death penalty for crimes committed while the perpetrator was under the age of sixteen.

It seems however that Stinney's case did not change the nation's conscience completely. Seventy people whose crimes were committed when they were minors are currently on death row in the US today.

This whole story seems to have been a rush to close a case. Eighty days from arrest to execution was very fast.

Lena Baker: A Miscarriage of Justice

Accused Name: Lena Baker
Crime: Murder
Conviction Date: April 30th, 1944
Execution Date: March 5th, 1945
Date Found Innocent: August 2005

Backstory of the Accused:
Lena Baker was born on June 8th, 1900. She was African-American, and her family was poor, working as sharecroppers, where they gave up a percentage of their crops in return for using someone else's land.

Baker grew up in the small community of Cotton Hill, close to the town of Cuthbert, Georgia. Her family moved to the area when she was a small child, and as she grew she too worked, chopping cotton for a local farmer. Baker lived with her parents, and also had a brother and two sisters.

When Baker was twenty, she and a friend found that money could be made 'entertaining gentlemen', as it was referred to during that time. However, in Georgia at the time, relationships between black and white people were illegal, and as they saw white clients, the pair was arrested and sent to the workhouse. Upon release, Baker found herself ostracized by her own community, and turned to alcohol. Over time, she became an alcoholic.

We know that by the time she was in her forties, Baker had three children of her own, worked as a maid, and also took in laundry. As well as supporting her own family, Baker helped to support her mother.

Description of the Crime:
In 1944, Ernest B. Knight, a white man, hired Baker to look after him while he recovered from a broken leg. He owned a local gristmill (a mill that grinds grains into flour), and his offer must have seemed like good fortune to Baker for the

money it would bring.

Knight was much older than Baker, twenty-three years her senior, and known by the community to be a heavy drinker with a bad temper, and to often carry a gun.

Despite the age difference, it's reported that it didn't take long for a sexual relationship to develop between the pair. There are rumors that Knight plied Baker with alcohol in exchange for sexual favors.

At one time, Knight's eldest son moved his father to Tallahassee, Florida, trying to end the relationship. Knight just brought Baker with him. When the son forced Baker to leave, Knight returned to Cuthbert with her.

After a time, Baker had a change of heart and tried to end the relationship. Rather than let her go quietly, it's reported that Knight responded by locking her in the mill against her will, for days at a time. There are some reports that say he used her for slave labor during this time.

As well as allegedly suffering physical abuse at Knight's hand, Baker reported that his son had also beaten her as a warning to stay away from his father. The sheriff also warned Baker that she was to stay away from Knight or he would throw her in jail. At the time Georgia was a heavily segregated state, and any relationship between a black and white person was illegal.

On April 30th, 1944, Baker arrived at the home of J.A. Cox, the town's coroner, and said to him that she had shot Knight. He told Baker that he would go and retrieve Knight's body, and she should go and tell the sheriff. Rather than inform local law enforcement, Baker went home.

That night the sheriff found her and picked her up. He ended up giving her two days to sleep off the effects of any alcohol in her system before interviewing her.

Evidence Used to Convict:
Baker told the sheriff that Knight had arrived at her house already drunk, and told her to accompany him to his mill. She didn't want to go, but too scared to refuse him, tried to buy herself some time by asking to go and buy whiskey first.

Knight gave her money, but when she arrived at the tavern in town she found it closed. She waited awhile before returning home. Knight was still there.

She told the sheriff that Knight forced her to go with him to the mill. On the way she escaped and was able to hide in the bushes. She then managed to buy her whiskey and spent the night at a convict camp nearby.

When she awoke the next morning, she decided to go to the mill, thinking that it was the last place Knight would go. By this time Baker had allegedly had a lot to drink.

When she found Knight at the mill, she was taken prisoner. Baker reported that Knight left for several hours, telling Baker on his return that he would kill her rather than let her leave him again. At the time, Knight was armed with a metal bar that he had used to keep the mill's doors closed.

His words provoked a struggle, with Baker making a grab for Knight's gun when he raised the bar over his head as if he meant to strike her. Baker claims that she was able to get her hands on his gun.

She said that the gun went off, shooting Knight in the head and killing him instantly. When asked who actually pulled the trigger, Baker replied that she didn't know.

Although Knight was not generally well liked, Baker's race worked against her. In a segregated society, a black woman killing a white man was not tolerated for any reason, no matter the feelings towards the actual persons involved.

Baker was charged with murder. Her trial started on August 14th, 1944. The presiding judge, William 'Two Gun' Worrill, was so named because he kept two pistols sitting in full view on his bench at all times. Judge Worrill was also vehemently pro-segregation.

Baker's trial lasted less than a day and was found guilty by a jury of twelve white men.

Typical of trials of African-Americans in segregated states in 1944, Baker was not allowed to testify in her own defense. In addition, her attorney did not call any witnesses. The all white jury delivered their verdict in just twenty minutes, a time that would be considered ludicrously fast by today's standards for a murder trial.

A court appointed attorney represented Baker. He filed her appeal, stating that the evidence presented could not support the verdict. He then immediately resigned as her lawyer. Because of his resignation, her appeal never made it beyond the county court.

A sixty-day reprieve was granted for the parole board to review her case. In January 1945, Baker was refused clemency. She was then transferred to the State Prison in February.

As she was strapped to the electric chair, Baker would only say that whatever she did, she did it in self-defense, to avoid being killed herself, and that she was ready to meet her God.

After her execution, Baker was laid to rest in an unmarked grave behind the church where she had been a member of the choir.

How Innocence Was Confirmed:
In 2003, Baker's great-nephew, Roosevelt Curry, formally requested a pardon from the State Board. The Prison and Jail Project, a Georgia prison advocacy board, assisted with the request.

A full and unconditional pardon was posthumously awarded by the State Board of Pardons and Paroles to Baker in August of 2005. In their decision, the board said that the decision in 1945 to deny Baker clemency was "a grievous error".

They also said that Baker could have been charged with manslaughter instead, which would have avoided a death sentence, carrying an average penalty of fifteen years.

Baker's nephew reportedly wept when he heard of the Board's decision, saying, "Now we can all cry tears of joy". Cole Vodicka, director of the Prison and Jail Project said that it was gratifying to see a blatant example of legal lynching and injustice finally recognized for what it had been.

The parole board said that the pardon was not a protest against racial injustice, or righting an historical wrong. Instead, they felt that the situation was unique and that it was a good thing to do for Baker's family.

They were clear to say that they did not find that Baker had been innocent, but instead the pardon was issued because she could have been charged with manslaughter instead. In her forties, Baker would likely have still been alive when released from jail.

Current Status:
Baker's story was made into a movie "Hope and Redemption: The Lena Baker Story" in 2009. Tichina Arnold starred as Lena.

Five decades after her death, the congregation from her church raised money to place a headstone on her grave. Her relatives met around the grave on Mothers Day 2001, and placed a floral wreath at Baker's final resting place.

They continued the tradition for years to come.

Baker remains the only woman executed by electric chair in Georgia. The old death chamber and the chair itself (grimly nicknamed Old Sparky) are now on display as a tourist attraction.

At the exhibit at a Georgia state prison, a photo of Baker along with her last words appears just near the electric chair that killed her.

Leo Alexander Jones: Justice Denied

Accused Name: Leo Alexander Jones
Crime: Murder of a Police Officer
Conviction Date: May 23rd, 1981
Execution Date: March 24th, 1998
Date Found Innocent: Never Officially Exonerated, Strongly Believed to be Innocent

Backstory of the Accused:
After extensive research, very little is known about Leo Alexander Jones except he was born on April 13th, 1950. He was a known drug dealer, having multiple arrests and convictions, one involving a shooting when he was just fifteen years old. According to his lawyers, he was well known in the neighborhood for his drug activities.

Description of the Crime:
On May 23rd, 1981, Jones was at home in his apartment with his cousin Bobby Hammond. The pair shared a place at 6th and Davis Streets, just a block from the interstate. At 1:10am two bullets were suddenly fired, one of which penetrated the windshield of a police cruiser while it was stopped at the intersection below Jones' apartment.

Police determined that the bullet had been shot from a .30-30 rifle. The bullet hit the wire cage separating the front and back seats, and a fragment ricocheted into patrolman Thomas Szafranski. The fragment hit him in the head, killing him. Szafranski was just twenty-eight years old.

Within minutes of Officer Szafranski's death, police were searching Jones' apartment building. It did not take them long to enter Jones' apartment, and he and Hammond were both taken in for questioning.

Police later released Hammond, but charged Jones, saying that he had confessed. Hammond also gave a statement saying that he saw Jones leave the apartment with a rifle, and shortly thereafter heard gunshots, Jones returning again shortly after that.

Evidence Used to Convict:
Even before his trial began, Jones' lawyer tried to have his confession thrown out, claiming that it was coerced. Jones claimed that police had beaten him and put a gun to his head, until he felt that he had no choice but to confess.

Supporting his statement was the fact that Jones had been taken to the hospital and treated for minor injuries at the time. A lawyer in the public defender's office also reported that he had seen Jones at a bond hearing shortly after he was arrested, and that at the time Jones had cuts and bruises on his face.

Jones' cousin, Hammond, recanted his own statement that he saw Jones with a gun, saying that officers had beaten it out of him, telling him to implicate Jones in the shooting.

Police testified that rather than being victims of police brutality, Jones and Hammond had in fact been injured while resisting arrest. They flat out denied that any physical abuse or coercion of any kind took place during their interrogations. A detective told the media that he simply talked to Jones until he was persuaded to confess.

Jones' lawyers also challenged the confession on the grounds that it was too vague in its description of the weapon, describing it only as a gun or rifle. The police told the court that they wrote only what Jones told them to write, and that he had voluntarily signed it.

The motion to throw out the confession was denied. When the murder trial started, Hammond
again changed his story, testifying against Jones. Jones himself claimed he was innocent, and was in bed when the shooting took place.

The prosecution argued that Jones was motivated by his hatred of police, and that Szafranski's murder was a revenge attack against an incident the week before, where Jones had been stopped by police.

The officer who stopped Jones at the time testified that Jones threatened to kill a police officer. However his report at the time made no mention of any such incident, and Jones denied it had ever taken place.

Two rifles that matched the description of the murder weapon were found in Jones' apartment. However one was ruled out using ballistic evidence, and the test on the second was found to be inconclusive.

Police did find Jones' fingerprints on one of the rifles. Jones however claimed that they belonged to another man Glenn Schofield to whom Jones had allegedly sold drugs that night.

Every member of the jury in Jones' trial was white, as was Officer Szafranski. One juror said after the trial that the evidence presented was 'pretty conclusive'. The evidence presented amounted to Hammond's testimony, Jones' alleged confession, and the discovery of the rifles in his apartment. No other evidence, including any forensic evidence definitively linking Jones to the murders was presented.

After convicting Jones, the jury voted nine to three in favor of the death penalty. Perhaps surprisingly, this vote does not have to be unanimous. The judge accepted the recommendation, and Jones was sentenced to death.

Jones' attorneys appealed the conviction, arguing again that the judge should not have let the jury hear his alleged confession. The law only allowed the appeal to focus on what happened during the trial, they were not allowed to introduce any new evidence. On this basis the appeal was denied. This continued for the next five years.

As time passed, Jones' lawyers started to discover new evidence. They faced a different and difficult legal standard to ask the court to reconsider the conviction. The state law at the time required that the evidence submitted not just raise doubts as to the jury's verdict, but be so compelling that a judge would have rendered the verdict a mistake and overridden the jury's decision.

Jones' lawyer, public defender Robert Link, discovered evidence of another man's involvement. He found witnesses that said the shot that killed Szafranski came from bushes in a vacant lot next door to Jones' building, and not from inside of it. The witnesses were listed on the police reports, but none of them had been called to testify at the original trial.

Jones' lawyer also started to look at the man who came to buy drugs from Jones that night, Glenn Schofield. He had denied any knowledge of the murder. When the lawyers looked into his background, they found a lengthy criminal record. In fact, Schofield had been in jail for all but three of the previous twenty-six years. He had earlier served five years for manslaughter, and had also been charged with murder in 1975.

It was discovered that just nine days after the murder of Szafranski, Schofield was involved in a bank robbery during which he shot a gun at police. He eventually pleaded guilty to a weapons charge, after first escaping from custody twice. He had then been paroled in 1989, only to be arrested on the same charge again.

In a review of the original police reports regarding Szafranski's murder, it was discovered that Schofield was also named as a suspect. He was dropped when Jones was arrested.

Anthony Hickson was a retired homicide detective who was a one-time partner with the officer leading Jones' investigation, Hugh Eason. Hickson came forward and reported that a confidential informant had told him it was Schofield who was responsible for Szafranski's murder all along. He says that he turned this evidence over to a lawyer for the defense after Jones' trial, but he would not identify his informant.

Jones' lawyer, Robert Link, began investigating and found other people who said that Schofield had told them he was the one who really killed Szafranski. Others could place him at the scene of the crime just moments before.

Link used these witnesses' testimony to appeal on the grounds that Jones' original attorney, H. Randolph Fallin, had been ineffective, as he had failed to locate these witnesses. However Fallin had a good reputation, and he testified that he had looked for witnesses in the local neighborhood, along with the help of Jones' family.

Once again, the appeal was denied by judge A. C. Soud, and then again in 1988 by the Florida Supreme Court. For its part, the state never changed its position, saying that Schofield was just running his mouth and was not truly involved.

In 1991, Jones' lawyers launched yet another appeal. This time, a girlfriend of Schofield testified that shortly after the murder, he told her to provide a false alibi for him and say she was with him when Szafranski was murdered. She also said that several years later Schofield bragged about being the true killer.

One of Jones' past girlfriends also testified, saying that she saw Schofield in the apartment building that night with a rifle. Two other witnesses signed affidavits that they saw Schofield running from the building with a rifle, shortly after hearing a shot. Jones' legal team also presented affidavits from three other inmates claiming that Schofield had bragged to them about being the killer.

Lastly, Hammond changed his mind again and signed an affidavit stating that he had in fact never seen Jones with a rifle.

Being so close to Jones' execution date, the appeal was heard on a Sunday afternoon. However, once again Judge Soud denied the appeal. He responded that the evidence presented was hearsay, and there was no other new evidence to support the claims. In his opinion, the fact that Schofield did not say these things until years later also weakened the statements.

Although in his particular case, the inmates that offered testimony and affidavits in support of Jones did not receive any particular benefits in return for their testimony, this can often occur. For this reason, testimony by inmates tends to be valued less than from those without a criminal record.

In the end, Soud stated that the defense had not overcome their burden, mainly due to a key point, Jones' confession. Soud said that he was unable to reconcile the confession with Jones' claims of innocence.

Jones' legal team did win a bittersweet victory. When the case reached the Florida Supreme Court, the court ruled that the current legal standard that new evidence had to be so strong as to demand a judge overrule a jury's verdict was almost impossible to meet. Instead, they said that the standard should be that newly discovered evidence should be strong enough only that in a new trial the likely verdict would be not guilty. As it was a decision of the state Supreme Court, this created a new law.

In Jones' case it did not matter. The court ruled that for various reasons, much of the evidence was not new. Some of the witnesses had been available for the original trial, while others had been already presented at an earlier appeal. Despite the new lower standard, with the loss of this evidence it was ruled that the appeal did not meet the criteria, and it was denied.

Jones' lawyers have told the media that they found the decision extremely frustrating. Legally, the appeal may have been successful if they had presented it in one shot much later in the case. However, given the severity of the sentence, his lawyers felt they were doing the right thing, trying to solve who truly killed Szafanski.

Despite this, another appeal was launched, with the discovery of another three new witnesses placing Schofield at the scene, including one who said he saw Schofield actually shoot the rifle from the empty lot. The Supreme Court would again decide against the appeal, saying that the evidence was redundant and non-persuasive. There was still no evidence to prove that Schofield did anything more than brag to many people. It is interesting to note, putting aside the troubling confession, that Jones' original trial also had little evidence.

Jones' legal team was not going to give up. A police officer who had retired in 1997, Cleveland Smith, came forward and claimed that another officer, Lynwood Mundy, bragged to him that he had beaten Jones after his arrest. Smith testified that Mundy had a reputation for such behavior, and that he had been extremely vivid in his descriptions of how he had beaten Jones.

Mundy's known behavior toward suspects included squeezing their genitals in a vice grip. Smith claimed he had waited so long to come forward because he wanted to secure his pension first. He testified that the culture of the Jacksonville police force made him fear reprisals if he had come forward earlier. The prosecution did not challenge Smith's credibility.

The detective in charge of Jones' case, Hugh Eason, also testified that at one time he had to drag Mundy off Jones while they were outside Jones' apartment. Mundy was interviewed at the time, but denied any misconduct. When Mundy left the police force in 1985, he was under suspicion for other incidents.

In 1982 two other police officers told an internal affairs investigation that Mundy had brought false charges against suspects, and had gone so far as to perjure himself in court hearings. One officer said that Mundy was an outright, known liar. Another internal affairs investigation in 1985 found that Mundy had roughed up a suspect. It was then that Mundy resigned.

Eason was also not above investigation. In 1987, prosecutors were investigating him for having a role in the murder of a used car lot owner. Evidence was presented to a grand jury, but charges were not filed. When Eason decided to retire later that year, the inquiry was closed.

Amazingly, a lawyer for the prosecution also had his own credibility issues. In 1985, Ralph N. Greene was indicted by a grand jury for conspiracy with a judge to intervene in cases involving friends. Green resigned during the trial, and was eventually acquitted.

Jones' final appeal was decided on March 17th, 1998. The majority of the bench of the Supreme Court now acknowledged that Schofield was potentially involved, but that at most the evidence suggested he might have been involved along with Jones.

Two judges were vigorous in their dissent, one listing at least twenty witnesses who either implicated Schofield or presented evidence that would have helped prove Jones' innocence. The judges believed this amount of evidence to be enormous and believed the court had been too restrictive, to the point of defeating justice. He went on to say that with inmate testimony being routinely used to secure convictions, it must be also equally valid to prove innocence.

Less than a week after the decision, Jones was executed. Over seventy police officers waited in the field across from the prison when the execution took place. Jones proclaimed his innocence to the end.

How Innocence Was Confirmed:
It is now believed by many that Jones was innocent of the charge, and that the real perpetrator was likely Schofield.

Despite the overwhelming amount of evidence presented at his multiple appeals, plus the evidence calling the reputation of members of the police force and a member of the prosecution team into question, Jones has never been officially pardoned or found not guilty.

Current Status:
A juror in Jones' original case had to pause and pull over to the side of the road when he heard on the radio that Jones had been executed. He recalled being so sure at trial, and that he had been impressed with the evidence the prosecution had presented.

As he heard more about the case over the years, he was no longer certain at all they had made the right decision. When Jones was finally executed, the juror felt that it all hit him at once, and he felt terrible.

Gary Graham: Guilty But Not of Murder?

Accused Name: Gary Lee Graham
Crime: Murder
Conviction Date: October 1981
Execution Date: June 22nd, 2000
Date Found Innocent: Never officially exonerated but widely believed to be innocent

Backstory of the Accused:
Gary Lee Graham was born on September 5th, 1963, to parents Thelma Griffin and Willie Graham. He had a rough start in life, his mother was seriously mentally ill and his father was a chronic alcoholic.

Graham recalled times that, as a small child, he had to chase his mother down the street when she fled the home completely naked. Other children in the neighborhood would laugh and make fun of her.

During his childhood, Graham's mother required repeated and extended periods of time in institutions for treatment of her mental illness. During this time, Graham lived with various relatives, and was often passed around from house to house.

As Graham grew, his father spent time in prison for years of his childhood. Graham ended up being raised mostly by his paternal grandmother, who also had a mental illness.

As he grew up, Graham's behavior became increasing negative. He dropped out of school in seventh grade, and was unable to read or write fully. At first he was involved in small, non-violent petty offenses, but by the age of seventeen he was arrested for his first felony crime.

During the week of May 14th through to May 20th, 1981, Graham committed at least nine different armed robberies against at least thirteen people. At all times he was armed with either a pistol or sawn-off shotgun. During the week Graham's crimes escalated in violence.

He shot one victim in the neck, struck a sixty-four year old man with the car he was stealing, and then abducted and held a fifty-seven year old woman for five hours, during which time he raped her.

Nineteen different eyewitnesses identified Graham as the perpetrator, and Graham was charged with ten armed robberies, and aggravated assault. He pleaded guilty, and was sentenced to twenty years in jail.

Description of the Crime:
Another case came to the attention of law enforcement. On May 13th, 1981, at approximately 9:30 in the evening, Bobby Grant Lambert was leaving a supermarket in Houston, Texas. Lambert was a fifty-three year old father and a resident of Tucson, Arizona. It is not known why he was in Texas. Lambert had also checked out of his hotel before visiting the store.

As Lambert was walking through the parking lot, someone approached him and put his hand in Lambert's back pocket. When Lambert resisted the attacker, a gun was held to his head. Lambert dropped his groceries, but the attacker still shot him through the chest and fled the scene.

Lambert was able to make it back inside the store, but died at the scene. The attacker managed to escape with just the change for the groceries from a $100 bill. Police later found $6000 on Lambert's body.

Evidence Used to Convict:
Previous robberies Graham had pleaded guilty to had also involved a gun (in his case usually a .22 caliber handgun), and had been committed between May 13th and 20th in the same area. Police were immediately suspicious of his involvement in Lambert's murder.

Investigators included Graham's arrest mug shot in the photo array shown to witnesses. One witness identified him as the perpetrator, and Graham was charged with capital murder.

Interestingly, although he had pleaded guilty to multiple other serious charges, Graham refused to admit guilt in this case, pleading not guilty to Lambert's murder.

The single witness to identify Graham was forty-five year old school clerk Bernadine Skillern, who had been sitting in her car in the parking lot at the time of the attack. She told police that the attacker had turned and looked at her when she sounded her horn as she saw the man put the gun to Lambert's head.

After Lambert was shot, she followed the attacker in her car until her upset children made her stop. She reportedly saw the man from 20-30 feet away and for around one and a half minutes.

Skillern picked out Graham's photo from a photo spread that included him and four other fill in photos. She also picked him out of a line-up the next day. She described the attacker as between eighteen and twenty years old, five foot ten inches to six feet tall, with a slim build and a close cut Afro. The description met Graham's appearance.

Graham's trial began in October 1981 in Harris County, Texas. In Texas a murder can qualify for the death penalty if it includes other certain circumstances. Examples of these include the murder of a police officer or fire fighter, the murder of multiple victims, murder for hire, or that the murder was committed during the course of another serious crime, such as in this case, robbery.

When a case of capital murder is tried, potential jurors are first questioned about their ability to consider the evidence and the ability to render a death sentence before they are even available for selection.

Similar to many Texas counties, there is no public defender system in Harris County. Instead, the judge appoints a private lawyer for defendants who cannot afford to hire one. Graham's appointed attorney was Ron Mock. Mock was very popular with the judges, and had been appointed to defend nearly ten percent of all capital cases in the county.

The fact that Mock was black, which was rare for a practicing lawyer in Texas in the 1980's, supports one theory as to why he was given so many of the capital cases. The judges were trying to promote diversity. He also owned a popular bar in the area, where judges and lawyers often drank.

Chester Thornton, who had represented him when he was a juvenile, and was also asked by Graham's family to represent him again.

At the time of Graham's trial, the district attorney was Johnny Holmes. Holmes had a reputation for seeking the death penalty in any case that was eligible. In fact, Harris County was the leader in issued death sentences across the entire USA. A full ten percent of all executions in the whole country were from Harris County cases.

The prosecution's case was built around the eyewitness testimony of Skillern. They also called two other witnesses who claimed that although they never got a good enough look at the perpetrator's face, Graham met the general description and could have been the attacker.

Most capital cases are actually decided without an eyewitness. In fact, defense attorneys have been quoted as saying they prefer it when there is an eyewitness, because it makes it easier to create reasonable doubt.

Unlike most other capital cases, in Graham's case there was little other evidence, physical or circumstantial. There was also no confession, making Skillern's identification crucial to the prosecution's case.

Graham's lawyers' defense was to dispute Skillern's identification. She had allegedly described the attacker before she was shown the photo array. Graham's photo was then the only one in the array that matched her description.

Further, he was the only person who was then included in both the photo array and the live line up. The defense argued that Skillern simply chose the only person who she recognized from the photo array, rather than the true murderer.

The judge ruled that Skillern had made her identification based solely on her independent recollections, and allowed her to testify. In response, the defense went on to make a point of the failure of the other witnesses to identify Graham. They did not cross-examine Skillern. The defense rested their case without presenting any further witnesses or evidence of their own.

The verdict was unanimous, Graham was found guilty 12-0.

The trial moved to the penalty phase. Unlike most states, where the jury makes the decision between execution and life in prison, in Texas the sentence is decided differently. Whether the case is eligible as a capital case is decided in the first stage of the trial, before the verdict has been rendered.

Three questions are asked;

Whether the defendant caused the death deliberately, and there are reasonable expectations that their actions would result in death.

Whether it was likely that the defendant would continue to commit criminal violent acts that would constitute a threat to society.

Whether the response of killing the victim was unreasonable in response to any provocation by the victim.

If the answer to those three questions is yes, the judge is required to sentence the defendant to death. There is no option for judicial or jury discretion.

The defense called members of Graham's family, who testified as to his difficult childhood, good character, and that he was generally non-violent. The prosecution was quick to point out his long juvenile record, that he was a high school drop out in the seventh grade, and had fathered two children already in his teens. Given his recent conviction for the string of violent robberies and rape, his fate seemed all but assured.

Despite the defense's pleas to take Graham's young age into account, he was sentenced to death at just eighteen years old.

It did not take long after his trial for claims of Graham's innocence and appeals to begin. Graham's supporters also claimed that his lawyer did not give him a proper defense. It has since been revealed that there were two eyewitnesses to the murder that, while they did not see the perpetrator clearly enough to identify him, both claimed that it could not have been Graham as the assailant was a maximum of five feet six inches tall. During Graham's original trial, his attorney did not call these witnesses.

Ballistic tests also showed that the gun Graham had in his possession when he was arrested was not the gun that killed Lambert.

Many famous anti death penalty activists became involved in protesting Graham's sentence, including Danny Glover, Jesse Jackson, and Al Sharpton. Many accused the Texas courts of discriminating against Graham based on race and class. The NAACP also filed a complaint with the U.S. Department of Justice on Graham's behalf.

In 1999, Graham called for his supporters to go to the prison where he would be put to death with AK-47 rifles to stop the execution. This likely did not help his cause. The leader of the Black Muslim Movement also urged young black people to take out their anger toward Graham's execution against white, wealthy neighborhoods.

While his trial may have had problems, neither was anything revealed in the early days after Graham's trial that categorically proved his innocence. At his original trial, Graham did not offer any credible alibi or explanation of his whereabouts on the night Lambert was killed.

He claimed that he had been with a girl, but could not remember her address, her name, or even her general appearance. Then, when his case was appealed, four different people offered alibis, including his wife. However, when she and another testified in front of a state district judge, they contradicted themselves and he deemed them not credible.

As it got closer to the date of Graham's execution, protests to save his live only grew in intensity. A full month of protests were held, planned to end in a large-scale protest outside of the execution chamber on the date of the execution itself.

Both sides of the legal system issued statements and evidence to support their position. Graham's lawyers even released signed affidavits from three of the original jurors, who said they had had a change of heart since the trial, after hearing about the two other eyewitnesses disputing the identification by Skillern. However, the prosecution fired back with an affidavit from a court bailiff, who as he escorted Graham from the courtroom, reportedly heard him say that next time, he would not leave any witnesses.

Incredibly, even Lambert's wife wrote a letter to the governor asking for the execution to be stayed. She said that she now believed that there was doubt as to whether or not Graham had committed the murder, and she did not want the murder of a possibly innocent man on her conscience.

There were still those who believed in Graham's guilt. Newspapers, in particular the Houston Chronicle, printed stories that included derogatory comments about Graham's claim to innocence. They also printed support for Graham's sentence from some of Lambert's family, and also from victims of the other crimes that Graham had pleaded guilty to.

In a speech a week before Graham's execution, the Attorney General said that the people of Texas could be assured that Graham had received the due process the American court system guarantees. He pointed out that the only case Graham was protesting his innocence in was Lambert's.

Graham had pleaded guilty to robbing thirteen victims over the course of a single week, including pistol-whipping two, shooting another in the neck, hitting a male victim with a car, and kidnapping and raping a female victim.

As well as Graham's guilty plea in those cases, three of Graham's other victims identified him as the perpetrator, along with a staggering nineteen eyewitnesses. He allegedly told Lisa Blackburn, the victim he raped, that he had already killed three other people and he was going to kill her too.

In Texas, the Governor may issue only one thirty day reprieve in a capital case, unless he has the support from the state Board of Pardons and Paroles in the form of a favorable recommendation.

Graham's lawyers had already petitioned the board for clemency two times, once in 1993 and then again in 2000. Both times the board denied any clemency in Graham's case. Despite the failed bid in 1993, then Governor Ann Richards granted Graham a thirty-day reprieve, stating she believed that there were questions that needed answering in the case.

Because of this, when a date was given for Graham's execution years later, then Governor George Bush was unable to grant another reprieve. That said, statements given by Bush indicate that he would not have granted one even if he were able. During Bush's time as governor, the board only spared a single prisoner.

On June 21st, 2000, Graham was moved to await his imminent execution. He resisted being moved, and multiple officers had to use shackles to control him enough to complete the transfer. Additional restraints and straps were used that are normally used in an execution.

Law enforcement was so concerned for the safety of residents and officials, that they closed the courthouse at noon that day, and business owners were advised to vacate the area. Prison workers living near the prison were told to leave and administrative staff was given the day off work.

That night, police set up barricades to separate the protestors. On one side were Graham's supporters and on the other was the Ku Klux Klan.

As a last minute attempt to save his life, Graham's lawyers had made multiple appeals and a habeas corpus petition with multiple courts. All failed. The next day at 5:30pm the U.S. Supreme Court issued a temporary stay. It would not last. Just a few hours later the court voted 5-4 to vacate the stay. By 8:49pm, Graham was dead. He was thirty-six years old.

How Innocence Was Confirmed:
Despite the doubts surrounding the case, and the unrelenting efforts of Graham's lawyers, he has never been be found innocent in the death of Lambert, or been issued an official pardon.

By the time of his execution, Graham's lawyers had lodged at least twenty appeals on his behalf, which had been heard and then rejected by over thirty-three different judges, from both state and federal courts.

Should very little evidence and one eye witness testimony be enough to put a man to death?

Current Status:
While in prison, Graham changed his name to Shaka Sankofa, and became a political activist. He chose the name Shaka to honor Shaka Zula, while the name Sankofa meant to go back to the past and bring to the present.

He co-founded a prison organization that was devoted to abolishing the death penalty, and wrote a book called *The Evolution of Shaka Sankofa*.

During his incarceration, he also gained his GED and a paralegal certification. He apologized to the victims of his spree of robberies.

More than two thousand people attended his wake and funeral. He was buried wearing a turquoise and gold African garment.

Graham's mother was found dead on the streets in 1988, just days after her latest release from the hospital. To their own dying day, both of his parents fought fiercely to try to free him from death row.

Graham's son was just two years old when Graham was arrested, and was arrested himself at age twenty for the murder of his friend, just three months before his father's execution.

He was convicted and sentenced to life in prison. He too claims he is innocent.

Carlos DeLuna: Possible Mistaken Identity

Accused Name: Carlos DeLuna
Crime: Murder
Conviction Date: July 1983
Execution Date: December 7th, 1989

Backstory of the Accused:
Carlos DeLuna was born on March 15th, 1962 to Maria DeLuna. His father is unknown. Carlos was a twenty-year-old Hispanic man from Corpus Christi, Texas. He dropped out of school in the eighth grade, and school reports commented that DeLuna was developmentally delayed.

Still only a young man, he had already been involved with the law, having been convicted of attempted rape, for which he served two years.

Description of the Crime:
On February 4th, 1983, twenty-four year old single mother Wanda Lopez was at her job as a gas station attendant in Corpus Christi, Texas. She had just called 911 for the second time to report a suspicious person, when she was attacked while she was still on the phone. She had already called 911 a short while earlier, but no one responded to the gas station until the end of her second call, at which time she was already in serious trouble.

Through a series of yes or no questions asked by the dispatcher, Lopez had identified her attacker as a Hispanic male. Listening to the tape transcript, it appears that Lopez was trying to give her attacker the store's cash, but she was still killed. Lopez was stabbed through her left breast with a knife, which police determined was a Buck knife. The wound hit an artery, and she bled to death at the scene.

A manhunt was quickly underway, and after just forty minutes, police found DeLuna hiding underneath a pickup truck. He was shirtless, wore no shoes, and was lying in a puddle of water. Police found a black wallet with just $2 inside, and a clump of bills totaling $149 inside his front pants pocket. DeLuna had recently been released from prison, and was breaking his parole by drinking in public. Police reports from that night list him as intoxicated to the point he was staggering.

DeLuna immediately told police that he had nothing to do with Lopez's death. He went so far as to offer to name another person that he had seen inside the gas station. He further claimed he had been in a bar over on the other side of the street.

Despite the fact that the attacker had struggled with Lopez and the crime scene was covered in blood, DeLuna's clothing and body was clean of any blood whatsoever. He would not have had time to clean up or change clothing.

Despite the lack of blood and his willingness to talk, DeLuna was arrested and placed in the back of a police cruiser.

Evidence Used to Convict:
Shortly after DeLuna was arrested, police made what many believe to be the first grievous mistake in the handling of the case. Police brought Kevan Baker, an eyewitness, to see DeLuna, who was shirtless and handcuffed in the back of a police car. Baker had seen a man struggling with Lopez inside the gas station. He described the man as dressed like a derelict, wearing a light colored shirt and dark pants, and had a moustache. Baker told police that the man had run off towards the northwest.

After the man ran off, he tried to assist Lopez until paramedics arrived. Police asked him if DeLuna was the killer while DeLuna was sitting handcuffed inside the police car, and Baker identified him as such. DeLuna had no moustache, wearing dress pants (he had also been wearing a white button-down shirt), and witnesses placed him east of the gas station.

Another eyewitness, George Aguirre, told police that he saw a man wearing blue or dark pants and a long sleeved t-shirt standing outside the gas station playing with a knife. The man approached Aguirre and asked for a lift, but nervous about the knife, he told the man no. He saw the man enter the gas station as he left.

Making a u-turn on the highway, Aguirre saw the man wresting with Lopez in the store. He pulled off the freeway and entered a nearby business to call the police. He returned to the gas station, where he identified DeLuna as the man with the knife.

Strangely he was not called at trial to identify him. Two other witnesses testified that they saw DeLuna jogging away from the gas station that night, wearing a white dress shirt and dark pants. They did not mention a knife, and the man they saw was clean-shaven.

At DeLuna's trial, the prosecution's argument was that he had stabbed and killed Lopez during the commission of a robbery. In Texas, this made it a possible death penalty case. The store manager testified that approximately $166 was missing from the inventory, having checked it himself four days prior. Typically it would only be off by $20-50.

There was no physical evidence of any kind linking DeLuna to the crime scene. The prosecution's evidence started with the 911 call indicating that a Hispanic male was the perpetrator. They also introduced Baker's identification of DeLuna.

At his trial, DeLuna finally named the man he had seen, calling him Carlos Hernandez. The prosecution argued that DeLuna had made up Hernandez, and claimed he didn't exist, calling him a phantom.

After DeLuna's lawyers passed on the name to the prosecution they went as far as to tell the court that the police had looked for someone named Carlos Hernandez but found no such person. They explained away the lack of blood on DeLuna's clothing, saying that it must have all washed away in the rain.

DeLuna did not help himself by claiming that earlier that night, before seeing Hernandez at the gas station, he had been at an ice skating rink, where he met Hernandez and his two sisters. At trial, one of the sisters said she had been at a baby shower that night, and not at the ice rink.

It took the jury just four and a half hours to find DeLuna guilty of capital murder. At the penalty part of his trial, they deliberated for six hours before deciding that DeLuna was likely to re-offend, based on his previous attempted rape conviction (where he broke three of the victim's ribs) and an earlier conviction for attempted rape.

As he had only been charged with misdemeanor assault at that time, DeLuna's lawyers had not fully investigated the charge, and say they were caught by surprise.

At no time during DeLuna's appeals was the question of innocence raised. Instead, his lawyers focused on appealing based on perceived errors in the law or handling of the case.
It's reported that even his own lawyers told the governor that he was guilty. In fact, one of DeLuna's lawyers, Hector De Pena, was the son of a local judge and former Deputy District Attorney and prosecutor.

Many believed he was placed as DeLuna's attorney as a favor to De Pena's father. De Pena has stated he believes that DeLuna and Hernandez committed the crime together, despite eyewitness testimony to the contrary. He has offered no evidence as to why he believes this.

DeLuna's other lawyer, Jimmy Lawrence, a more seasoned defense attorney, does not believe that DeLuna was innocent either. He has been quoted as saying 'of course he was guilty'. He is bothered to this day why DeLuna refused to identify Hernandez from photographs, not understanding why DeLuna would not help himself when his life was on the line.

How Innocence Was Confirmed:
DeLuna's case is perhaps one of the most well known for the execution of an innocent man, despite the fact that he has never officially been pardoned. In 2012, an over 400-page report was published in a human rights law review by Columbia Law School professor James Liebman, along with his students.

The professor spent four and a half years reviewing evidence before publication. He believes that there is no doubt that Texas executed an innocent man. The Columbia Human Rights Law Review cleared its entire spring edition to run the piece, double the regular entire size of the publication.

Professor Lieberman and his students interviewed more than one hundred witnesses, and re-examined over nine hundred pieces of evidence, source material, and crime scene photos before writing the book-sized document.

From the moment he was arrested, DeLuna claimed that he hid under his truck when he heard the police sirens because he was on parole and got scared. Was the only true eyewitness therefore the couple who saw a clean-shaven Hispanic man in a white shirt near the scene without any weapon?

Baker has since told the media that he was never absolutely sure that DeLuna was the true attacker, and that he only indicated he was when it had already been hinted at by police that he was. In fact, he is quoted as saying that if he had not been told by police he had been arrested in the area, he would have only been 50% sure he even had the right man.

Along with the lack of blood on DeLuna's clothing, there was other troubling handling of forensic evidence. The crime scene was very quickly turned back over to the gas station owner. He has said that he was stunned to be handed back control of the scene and told he could wash the blood away just two hours after a major felony.

Police took photos of the crime scene, one of which shows a partial shoe print framed in blood. Lopez was barefoot when she had been murdered, and so the print had to have come from the killer, yet there was no blood on DeLuna's shoes.

Police also found a cigarette butt near the victim. The brand was one that Hernandez smoked. Lastly, police found a red button. Baker mentioned to police that the killer wore a dark red suit. Hernandez wore a red flannel shirt so often at that time of year that friends called it his winter uniform.

None of these items were taken from the crime scene and stored as evidence, including a sample from the bloody footprint. No blood samples were ever tested against DeLuna's blood type, nor were any of the other items forensically tested.

Other photographs of the scene show lead investigators standing on physical evidence. Four fingerprints were found at the scene, none of which matched DeLuna. In fact, they had been so poorly lifted they could not be used at all. Lastly, no fingernail scrapings were taken from the victim, despite the attack happening in close quarters.

Not only was no blood visually evident on DeLuna's clothes, when they were tested in a lab, not a single microscopic droplet was found. The prosecution's explanation that the rain must have washed it all away is nearly laughable with what we know today.

When Liebman asked for access to the evidence to test it with technology that was not available in 1983, he was told that it had all disappeared, every single piece.

DeLuna's case had become a death penalty case due to the prosecution's claim that Lopez's death occurred during the commission of another crime, the robbery. However, it is not known if money was truly taken from the store, and there was no other evidence elevating it to a capital case.

The store manager has since said, over twenty years later, that in fact it would not have been unusual for the store to be $166 down from the last count. In addition, Lopez would have likely had no more than $75 in the drawer at the time of the attack in the first place. The money found crumpled up in DeLuna's pants therefore is likely completely unrelated to the case.

Interestingly, neighbors of Hernandez said that he and Lopez were romantically involved. Was Lopez's death the result of a fight between lovers? There's no evidence that DeLuna and Lopez ever knew each other.

Hernandez was a well-known criminal in the town. He had a moustache (as Baker first noticed about the man in the store), and had a habit of dressing like a hobo (Baker described the attacker's dress as derelict) and carrying a knife.

Physically, DeLuna and Hernandez looked incredibly similar. They were both 5 foot 8 inches, both weighed 160 pounds, and had wavy black hair.

Photos of each Carlos shown to relatives of the other were even mistaken for their own relative. While both men had been arrested during their lifetime, DeLuna's criminal record did not contain any crimes using weapons.

His most serious crime was an attempted rape, for which he served the two years jail. Hernandez's crimes, on the other hand, often involved a knife.

In fact, just days before Lopez's murder, Hernandez was picked up hiding out behind a 7-11 store with a knife. Several of his crimes involved robberies of gas stations in the town. Neither of these facts was disclosed at DeLuna's trial.

It's since been revealed that a police informant told a detective that Hernandez was Lopez's killer. We now also know that not only were the police told about Hernandez's likely involvement, but one of the prosecutor's in DeLuna's case knew Hernandez intimately.

Just three years before DeLuna's trial, he had interviewed Hernandez in relation to the stabbing death of another young Hispanic woman. When he was arrested for that crime, Hernandez had been carrying a Buck knife.

And yet at trial they denied all knowledge that Hernandez even existed. The prosecution has since admitted they should not have said that Hernandez was a phantom at court.

It is now known that police investigated Hernandez for the crime before DeLuna ever accused him in his own trial. In fact, over his adult life Hernandez was arrested thirty-nine times, but almost never imprisoned. Leibman believes this is because he was used as a police informant.

Incredibly, just two months before DeLuna was executed, Hernandez was sentenced to ten years in prison for attempted murder of a Hispanic woman. The weapon used was a knife, but still no one put two and two together. How could the authorities have missed this?

Current Status:
From the moment he was arrested until his dying breath, DeLuna never wavered from protesting his innocence.

When Professor Liebman first heard about DeLuna's case, he thought that it looked like any other routine, everyday case, but then he heard the name Carlos Hernandez almost mentioned in passing in relation to DeLuna's case. He paid a private investigator to spend just a single day looking for any sign of a man named Carlos Hernandez.

In that one day, the investigator uncovered evidence that was either undiscovered or ignored for over six years by scores of police, prosecutors, defense lawyers, and judges. Liebman is now highly critical of the death penalty, saying that if on the surface a case like DeLuna's could look completely normal, how many other innocents have been executed in the name of justice?

After reviewing the information uncovered, Lopez's own brother, Richard Lopez, issued a statement saying that he no longer believes that DeLuna killed his sister, and that the real perpetrator was Hernandez.

District Attorney Mark Skurka, who has not read the journal report, and police investigator Paul Rivera, who has reviewed the police and trial records, both still believe DeLuna was guilty.

Hernandez allegedly told many relatives about the stupid "tocayo" that had gone to prison in his place. Tocayo is a Spanish word for namesake. He would die in prison of cirrhosis of the liver ten years after DeLuna was executed.

Before he died, he stabbed a Hispanic woman nearly to death, and was arrested a further five times. When he died in prison, he was serving a sentence for assault with a knife.

With the lack of evidence pointing to DeLuna and Hernandez' prison confession, was a man wrongly executed?

Ruben Cantu: Victim of False Testimony

Accused Name: Ruben Cantu
Crime: Murder
Conviction Date: November 4th, 1984
Execution Date: August 24th, 1993

Backstory of the Accused:
Ruben Cantu was born in Texas on December 5th, 1966. He was the fourth of five children born to his parents, Fidencio (Fred) and Aurelia Cantu. His was an unusual family, his mother marrying a man over two decades older than her when she was just thirteen years old.

Cantu's father worked long hours as a maintenance man, and so when she was barely a child herself, Aurelia raised her children predominantly on her own. Cantu would often watch TV until well after midnight, and is remembered as an easy, eager to please child.

He lived with both his parents until the age of fourteen, when his parents separated. His mother moved twenty miles away. Cantu's mother reportedly asked him to move with her, but he chose to stay with his father.

The pair lived in a trailer in a crime-filled neighborhood. Fred Cantu continued to work long hours, and Cantu was left alone long into the night. He started skipping school, and soon became involved with questionable activities. He ended up dropping out in the ninth grade.

The neighborhood where Cantu lived was home to an informal gang, really a group of tough kids calling themselves the Grey Eagles. Despite his small stature, and being involved in special education classes at school, Cantu became the leader of the group. Before long, he was sampling illegal drugs.

His life changed quickly after that, and by the time he was

fifteen years old he was involved in an organized car theft racket. Rather than attend school, he spent days at a time driving stolen cars to Mexico. Growing up in poverty, Cantu suddenly could spend all he wanted on games, movies and more drugs.

At that time, the San Antonio police department was in the middle of a scandal. Both vigilante cops and drug-dealing officers were well known in the local community. Cantu's older brother had also been arrested on drug related charges, and so Cantu had grown up knowing that no matter what, you could never trust the police.

Despite his lifestyle, Cantu's own record remained clean. Police knew who he was and they shared a mutual distrust, but they had never been able to pin him for a crime. That is, until that one fatal night that would change his life.

Description of the Crime:

On November 8th, 1984, at approximately 11:30pm, two men broke into a house in San Antonio, Texas. The house was vacant and currently undergoing construction. At the site were two guards, Pedro Gomez and Juan Moreno. Moreno was the brother of the owner.

They were also workmen on the site during the day, and had been sleeping on mattresses at the site overnight to guard against theft, after a few pieces of equipment had been stolen from the job site. Gomez had a gun hidden under his mattress. The only light in the property was from a small lamp plugged into the neighbor's outlet, and there was no running water.

That night, the lamp being switched on awakened Gomez and Moreno. They came face to face with two Latino teenagers, one of them brandishing a .22 caliber rifle. First, the teens took their watches, and when they tried to rob the men of their cash (still in their pockets from the day's work), Gomez handed over his wallet before attempting to reach for his gun.

One of the perpetrators then reacted and shot Gomez at least nine times, following swiftly with multiple shots aimed at Moreno. Thinking that both men were dead, the perpetrators fled the scene. Gomez had died instantly but Moreno was still alive and would survive the attack.

After the two men left, Moreno was able to leave the house in search of help. Police found him just before midnight, bleeding all over the seat of a pick-up truck parked in front of the house. He could say only that two Latino teens had attacked them, and he thought they lived nearby.

Evidence Used to Convict:
A police officer attempted to visit Moreno in the hospital the next day, but Moreno was unable to move, let alone speak, due to the severity of his injuries. Another five days would pass, and police visited Moreno in the hospital again. Moreno could still barely talk, and could say only that he thought one of the teens was around 14 and the other 19.

A rumor started circulating at a school in the neighborhood. A shop teacher had heard that three local kids had been involved in the robbery and murder, and Cantu was mentioned as being one of them. He lived across the street from the vacant house where the attack took place and was known to police as a troublemaker.

Police visited Moreno again on December 16th, over a month since the incident, and this time showed him a photo array that included Cantu. At that time, Moreno did not identify Cantu, or anyone else for that matter, from the five photos. The case grew cold and stayed that way for four months.

On March 1st, 1985 another incident occurred. Cantu shot off-duty police officer Joe De La Luz at a bar. Cantu said that De La Luz threatened him, including revealing his concealed weapon, but did not identify himself as a police officer.

Scared, Cantu fired first and shot De La Luz four times. De La Luz however said that Cantu fired with no cause or provocation. De La Luz survived, and eventually the case against Cantu was dropped, as police had conducted an illegal search at Cantu's home.

Bill Ewell, a friend of De La Luz worked in homicide and after the shooting of his friend he decided to immediately reopen the murder investigation into the construction site shootings, taking a closer look at Cantu.

Police visited Moreno again with a photo array that included Cantu. Once again, Moreno could not identify Cantu as the man who shot him. He did identify him by name to the police, and also learned that he had shot a police officer.

At this point in the investigation, it's important to note that Moreno was an undocumented Mexican immigrant.

The next day Moreno was again visited by the police. This time, he was taken to the police station, sat down, and shown the same photo array again, which by now Moreno had viewed three times. This time, he identified Cantu as the one who shot him and Gomez.

Cantu was arrested along with his alleged accomplice, friend David Garza, who was fifteen. Garza pleaded guilty, but Cantu decided to go to trial.

In Cantu's trial, the prosecution's entire case was Moreno's identification. There was no confession, no murder weapon was ever found, and there was not a single shred of forensic evidence linking Cantu to the crime. David Garza, Cantu's friend, refused to implicate Cantu.

Prosecutor Bruce Baxter interviewed Moreno before the trial, and believed him to be sincere in his identification. He knew Moreno, a teen himself at nineteen, and so badly injured, would be able to garner great sympathy from the jury.

During trial, Moreno delivered a heart wrenching testimony about how he watched his friend shot and then nearly died himself.

Cantu's lawyer, Andrew Carruthers, was an experienced lawyer, but he had never been involved in a death penalty case. His defense was to try to discredit Moreno, but it didn't work. Cantu was found guilty.

The trial moved to the sentencing phase, and prosecutors called De La Luz. The police officer testified that Cantu had shot him without provocation. Without his testimony, prosecution would have been left with only vague rumors of Cantu's alleged gang activity and drug possession. Texas law requirement that the defendant was likely to continue to commit violent criminal acts would not have been met for a capital case.

Cantu himself was told by his lawyer not to testify, so he sat quietly in the courtroom for the entire trial. When he was condemned to die, he broke down and wept. At the time of the crime, Cantu was just seventeen years old.

After being convicted, Cantu wrote a note to the city, saying that he had been framed because he shot an off-duty police officer.

Cantu was executed by lethal injection on August 24th, 1993. When he died, he was twenty-six years old.

How Innocence Was Confirmed:

Cantu's attorney's appealed, based on the reliability of

Moreno's identification. In his first appeal, even the Court of Criminal Appeals ruled that the identification had been improperly leading, but they did not overturn Cantu's conviction.

Assuming that Moreno had returned to Mexico, not one of Cantu's lawyers attempted to find him and ask him for themselves if Cantu was indeed guilty.

Cantu claimed that on the day of the crime he was miles away in Waco, stealing a truck with another friend. However, according to official records no record of the theft of the truck was ever recorded.

In 2003, more than ten years after Cantu was executed, the Houston Chronicle published a dossier, including sworn statements and retracted testimonies, and stated that Cantu should never have been charged with capital murder, let alone convicted.

Moreno, who had never gone back to Mexico and still lived in a suburb of San Antonio, recanted his statement naming Cantu as the shooter, saying years later that he felt pressured by police due to his own immigration status.

He says he was never shown a photo of the true killer, and that in part because of his testimony, an innocent man was executed.

Cantu's co-defendant, Garza, signed a sworn affidavit saying that he allowed his friend to be falsely accused, and that Cantu was not with him the night the shooting took place. He says that instead he was with another, unnamed teen.

Without a single piece of forensic or other evidence against Cantu, and the two witnesses now saying Cantu was not involved, the case against him today would not exist.

Many now believe that Cantu was completely innocent of the crime, and setup to take the fall because the police couldn't pin him for the shooting of one of their own, De La Luz. Cantu has never been officially pardoned.

Current Status:
Moreno says he still feels pain from his injuries on that night, and is still traumatized by seeing Gomez die in front of his eyes. A San Antonio District Attorney has threatened to charge him with murder by perjury.

Garza told the media that on the night of Cantu's execution, he listened to the news report on the radio in his cell, and wept for things left unsaid.

The district attorney who made the decision to seek the death penalty in Cantu's case says now in hindsight it should never have even been an option.

Did the Judicial System let Cantu down?

Conclusion

These are not by far the only cases of wrongful executions. They are merely a selection made to exemplify the timing, reasons, prevailing social norms and the errors and ineptitude that caused these people to lose their lives.

Laws have been enacted that prohibit executing a person with mental disabilities and juveniles under the age of 16. Also, the length of time people are allowed to be on death row and submit appeals has become years or decades long.

Executed Unjustly brings to light the circumstances under which these people were put to death, but is not a comment on the ethics of the death penalty. Individuals need to decide that for themselves.

Thank You

Dear Readers,

Thank you for buying and reading my book. I hope you found it interesting and thought provoking.

If you enjoy reading about true crime, please check out my other books, listed at the beginning of the book.

Thank you again and pleasant reading,

Mike Riley

15664778R00047

Printed in Great Britain
by Amazon